Your Amazing Itty Bitty Dissertation Book
15 Simple Steps to Write Your Dissertation

You belong to the few students who decide to run the doctoral race but you may have underestimated the planning and preparation for this research and writing marathon. Lack of clear guidance and support often leads to a long and frustrating process. This book provides you with specific steps and ideas to conquer the doctoral journey and graduate with your capstone title.

Questions students ask:

- How do I pick a topic?
- How to I start research?
- What elements belong into a proposal and into a dissertation?

If you are considering a PhD or are already on your way, pick up a copy of this stimulating book today and find strategies to complete your doctorate degree successfully!

Your Amazing Itty Bitty™

Dissertation Book

15 Simple Steps to Write your Dissertation

Dr. Laura Haase
Dr. Anja Thelen

Published by Itty Bitty™ Publishing
A subsidiary of S & P Productions, Inc.

Copyright © 2016 Laura Haase & Anja Thelen

All rights reserved. No part of this book may be reproduced or transmitted in any form or by any means, electronic or mechanical, including photocopying, recording or by any information storage and retrieval system, without written permission of the publisher, except for inclusion of brief quotations in a review.

Printed in the United States of America

Itty Bitty™ Publishing
311 Main Street, Suite E
El Segundo, CA 90245
(310) 640-8885

ISBN: 978-1-931191-83-8

To all those students who need a helping hand.

Stop by our Itty Bitty™ website to find interesting blog entries regarding Your Amazing Doctoral Dissertation.

www.IttyBittyPublishing.com

or contact us at

www.graduatedegreecoaches.com

Table of Contents

- Step 1. Create or Discover Your Topic
- Step 2. Evaluate Your Access to People and Data
- Step 3. How to get Started Writing
- Step 4. Research
- Step 5. Reevaluate
- Step 6. Overall Proposal Content Guide – Generic
- Step 7. Your University Guide or Template for Content
- Step 8. Chapter 1 - Problem Statement and Research Questions/Hypothesis
- Step 9. Chapter 2 - Literature Review
- Step 10. Chapter 3 – Methodology
- Step 11. Editing
- Step 12. Overall Dissertation Content Guide/Results
- Step 13. Chapter 4 - Data Analysis
- Step 14. Chapter 5 - Findings/Themes - Future Research
- Step 15. Editing Again

Introduction

In this Itty Bitty™ Book you will find 15 simple things you can do to write and finish your dissertation. The authors of this book went through some tough times to start and finish their dissertations. The process was painful because information about the structure and elements was not available or not available in an understandable way. The final push came through the identification of a mentor who helped each of us through the process. This book cannot replace a mentor, but it can get you on the right track by giving you the elements your dissertation needs, and tips and tricks to finish.

Simple Steps

Step 1
Create or Discover Your Topic

In this Itty Bitty™ Book you will find 15 simple things you can do to increase your success rate at completing your dissertation and actually enjoy the journey!

1. Now that you have decided to pursue your PhD, it is time to learn how to move forward toward completing your dissertation!
2. Pick a topic that really interests you, as you will be writing about it for some time!
3. Solve one problem - not all of them!
4. Remember you are adding a brick to the Great Wall of Knowledge, not creating an entire new wall.

Topic Selection

- Pick a topic area that interests you!
- Within the topic area, pick a problem you want to solve or a topic area needing more research.
- Make sure you are not writing about a topic that is already part of the existing body of knowledge. For example: Children in low socio-economic conditions do not do as well in school as children in high socio-economic conditions. This general topic has been researched to extreme, so how is your study different?
- What is missing in the research that interests you and how can you create a study around it?
- Find a dissertation partner, preferably someone just starting out in your same discipline, and help each other through the program. This gives you someone to relate to who knows the struggles of the program and workload! The best place to work with a dissertation partner would be in person, but you can also use online groups and resources.

Step 2
Evaluate Your Access to People and Data

Now that you have an idea about your topic, it is time to see if your proposed research is something you can carry to the end of the process! For example, are you looking to write about the CIA, but you do not work for the CIA or have access to people who do? If so, you may want to pick another topic.

1. Be realistic about your access to participants (i.e., you cannot interview people about top-secret information and print it).
2. Consider realistically if you can get access to the location you want to research. Some organizations may have their own processes for giving you rights to do research.
3. Qualitative research generally involves interviewing or using questionnaires with people to learn about their experiences.
4. Quantitative research generally deals with a large volume of data and statistical analysis.
5. Mixed methodology combines both qualitative and quantitative research.
6. For more information on the different types of studies, see the next page.

Resources for Methodology

Each methodology has many facets and an in-depth explanation would take another entire book.

- Check with your university, university library, and mentor to find information about the different methodologies for qualitative, quantitative, and mixed methods studies.
- Read about the different methodologies.
- **Check with your mentor for the best method for your study.**
- Use the following link to find information for the major qualitative and quantitative research, as well as courses: www.graduatedegreecoaches.com

Step 3
How to Get Started Writing

Create an outline - spend time looking at other dissertations in your field and at your University template for writing a dissertation.

1. See Step 6 for a sample of a generic (qualitative and quantitative) dissertation outline.
2. Pull peer reviewed articles from major research databases such as ProQuest, EBSCO, and Google Scholar.
3. Read as many research articles (peer reviewed articles, conference papers, and dissertations) as you can in your area and jot down thoughts, connections, and ideas for topics.
4. Write for 30 minutes every day no matter what you write! Yes, we encourage you to write around your topic but if nothing comes to mind write what is on your mind. It is much easier to edit existing work than to stare at a blank page!
5. Do not worry about perfecting the work; that will come with time!
6. Alignment - the centerpiece of your work! Please check www.graduatedegreecoaches.com and the next page for resources and worksheets!

Ideas and Resources for Getting Started Writing

- Create a space for writing: Organize your work area and have all your tools available. Make sure it is not cluttered, but do not spend your time every day on cleaning it – keep it clean!
- Create time for writing: Write out your daily/weekly tasks and identify times where you can work on your dissertation. Don't even think of scheduling a whole day just for writing – start with15-30 minutes per day. Put the time you selected in your calendar and stick to it!
- Writing consists of reading and reflecting on something and then creating ideas and thoughts around it, revising those thoughts and sentences, and editing multiple times thereafter.
- The process of writing can seem daunting. It can help if you make a journal and jot down your thoughts about a specific topic without making it sound "scholarly."
- Create an outline of your thoughts – "the red thread" going through your dissertation.

Step 4
Research

Starting your research may seem like a daunting task in the beginning, but it can be a lot of fun. Proceed step-by-step and try not to get overwhelmed.

1. Collect relevant papers you read and create a table, mind map, or folder to find similarities and differences between the authors and their findings. Find the authors these authors are citing (seminal research) and their original perspectives.
2. Don't just read the articles; for later use it is helpful to create an annotated bibliography for each article you read. See www.graduatedegreecoaches.com for ways to summarize and an example of an annotated bibliography.
3. Jot down the answers to the following questions: Who are the authors (their experiences and credentials) and do their perspectives align with your research? Who is opposing your perspective? What methodology did they select and what subjects did they focus on?

You can find more information and courses on: www.graduatedegreecoaches.com.

Keep Your Documents Organized and Safe...

- Throughout your coursework, keep all articles and books you are required to read or find during your research and writing – they may be usable for your dissertation.
- Make sure you download and save any article, dissertation, paper, and website to a folder for your research.
- Create a reference library in the format your dissertation has to follow (e.g. APA, Chicago, MLA) either in a Word, Excel, or database program that suits your needs (examples are EndNote, CiteFast, Zotero, and Mendeley). This will come in handy during your studies and during your dissertation writing.
- Organize your research, either in folders on your computer, or by adding keywords to your reference library, or any other type of organization you wish.
- Make regular backups of your educational and dissertation folders on an external hard drive, flash-drive, in an online cloud-service, and/or your email folder. You do not want to lose all your research and writing – it always happens at the worst moment!

Step 5
Reevaluate

At this point, you have most likely spent quite some time refining your search for literature, reading and summarizing. Let's say you have 30-50 articles in your library and now it's time for a reevaluation. Lay out all your notes and look at what you have written down in Step 1 and 2.

1. Have you found an answer to your question or problem in these articles? If yes, then you need to find a different topic or question. If not, continue your evaluation.
2. Did other researchers suggest additional research about the topic/problem? If not, why not, in your opinion? There may be a reason for this and you would need to argue in your proposal why you still want to research this topic/problem. If yes, continue your evaluation.
3. What areas of research were suggested? How does your topic/question fit into these requests?
4. Is the topic/problem/question you asked in Step 1 and 2 still current or did it evolve?
Remember: You do not want your topic to become broader – rather you want to narrow it down as small as you can!

Laying Out Your Current Research Status

- Laying out your current research allows you to see the literature you have collected, the areas you have studied, and what areas may need further research. The idea is to oversee what you know, when, and who it is from, as well as what matches, what opposes, and what is missing to create a rounded view of the topic you study.
- Reevaluation helps you to keep on track with what you want to research and not lose your focus. The process of reevaluation also helps you write parts of Chapters 1 and 2 in your dissertation – so it's essential to keep good notes. Reflecting on the process in your writing journal can help you write these sections later (see Step 3).
- Now create a schedule when you want to accomplish which sections to write next in your dissertation. You do not have to go linear through the chapters - align it with your own writing style and allow for jumps and revisions.

Step 6
Overall Proposal Content Guide - Generic

The following is a basic outline of the dissertation proposal, Chapters 1 through 3:

1. Chapter 1: Introduction
   This chapter includes the introduction to the study, the background of the study, the problem statement, a short overview of the gap in literature, the purpose and significance of the study, your research question(s), definitions, and a summary.
2. Chapter 2: Literature Review
   This chapter includes information about your researched literature, documentation, a discussion of differing perspectives on your topic (sorted, for example, from historic to current information), gaps in identified research, a conclusion, and a summary.
3. Chapter 3: Research Method
   This chapter includes a description of the research method and design, including a comparison of methods and reasoning for the selection, a description of the sample and its characteristics, your research and interview questions and how you constructed them, a discussion about how the data collection process and analysis process will be structured, and a summary.

How to Structure Your Proposal

- Create a document outline of your Chapters 1 through 3 and what topics and sub-topics you may want to write about.
- Your proposal has more detail in certain areas than your final dissertation will have.
- Be explicit on how you will research your topic.
- Describe your sample, characteristics, and size in detail:
    - How will you protect your participants, the data you collected, confidentiality?
    - How will you collect informed consent?
    - How will you analyze the data?
    - How will you present the data?
- Add all documents/forms you will use during your data collection:
    - Permission to use premises, names, and/or subjects.
    - Invitations/letters to participate.
    - Informed consent.
    - Proposed interview protocol.
    - Proposed interview questions.
- Anything else you may use/need.

Step 7
Your University Guide or Template for Content

Identify your template for your dissertation from your university. Check multiple sources, including the (online) library and writing centers, your doctoral homepage, as well as graduate templates to identify the templates required for you.

1. Lay out the templates for:
    a. your dissertation.
    b. the writing standard used (e.g. APA, Chicago, MPA).
    c. common mistakes you have made in previous writings.
2. Open an empty word-processing document on your computer or use the university-provided template.
3. Adjust the document step-by-step to the requirements for your doctorate-level document.
4. If you are not using certain information (e.g. tables, heading…), write the information in a section within the document and review it later.

What to Adjust in Your Doctoral Template Document

- Margins
- Headings
- Fonts and font-size
- Paragraph and sentence spacing
- Headings
- Table example
- Table of contents
- Table of figures and tables
- Pagination
- Running titles
- Reference lists
- Appendix

An Ongoing Process…

- Adjusting your template may not be a one-time action – some universities change their format and you will need to review the guidelines right before you submit – but it will be much easier if you have formatted the document early.
- Citation requirements may change, too. Get started early and keep up-to-date with changes.

Step 8
Chapter 1 - Problem Statement and Research Questions/Hypothesis

The full outline of the chapter depends on your universities' guidelines and on the methodology you will be using. The following items are listed here with numbers, but are not numbered in your dissertation. Basic ingredients include:

Chapter 1: Introduction
1. Introduction
2. Background of the Study
3. Purpose of the Study – The purpose is…
4. Problem Statement – The problem is…
5. Gap in Literature (this should only be a short overview, the main part will be in Chapter 2)
6. Research Question(s)/Hypothesis – appropriate to your methodology
7. Significance
8. Alignment of Research Question, Purpose, Research Design, and Study Questions
9. Scope and Limitations you can already preempt
10. Theoretical Framework (this should only be a short overview, the main part will be in Chapter 2)
11. What you expect to contribute to the body of knowledge
12. Definitions
13. Summary

Tips for Chapter 1

- Start with an outline of the different headings and create subheadings.
- Fill the areas with your current information and knowledge.
- Create a dictionary for words and abbreviations. From these you can then decide which ones are most important and go into your terms or definitions section in Chapter 1.
- Provide expanded definitions for your most important words/terms/concepts.
- Do not try to get it perfect the first time around – you will gather additional knowledge and insight from writing Chapters 2 and 3. (Return to Chapter 1 after you have written these chapters and edit and expand your writing.)
- Make sure you hit the points your university asks for.

Step 9
Chapter 2 - Literature Review

The full outline of the chapter depends on your universities' guidelines and on the methodology you will be using. The following items are listed here with numbers, but are not numbered in your dissertation. Basic ingredients include:

Chapter 2: Literature Review
1. Discussion how and where you found your scholarly resources
2. Depending on your topic, provide --
    a. Historic and current perspectives of your topic (aka subheadings)
    b. Focus on differing perspectives/authors/ideas/ frameworks
3. A discussion about most important factors, systems, etc.
4. Theoretical Framework (if applicable)
5. Explain the current gaps in research
6. Literature Conclusion
7. Summary

Tips for Chapter 2

- Develop headings and subheadings – you can always merge information later.
- Use your list of journals, papers, and books to create an annotated bibliography. This will help you to find "fitting" areas in your subheadings, where you discuss the findings.
- Find the seminal work.
- Chapter 2 is not a list of literature you found and find interesting. You need to highlight similarities and differences between different authors, their research and how they relate to your topic. This can include differing frameworks, use of words, techniques, and more.
- Also, be sure to cover those authors who do not agree with the majority of the authors on your topic, in order to show both sides of the issue.
- If you are using one or more theoretical frameworks – this is the place to describe them and to reason why one is your focus or not.
- Make sure to pay attention to readability of a person who is not an expert in your subject area.

Step 10
Chapter 3 - Methodology

The full outline of the chapter depends on your universities' guidelines and on the methodology you will be using. The following items are listed here with numbers, but are not numbered in your dissertation. Commonly used sections include:

Chapter 3: Research Method

1. Research Method and Design description
2. Sample and Characteristics
3. Research and Interview Questions/Survey quantitative instrument use
4. Privacy and Security
5. Data Collection Process
6. Data Analysis Description
7. Summary

Tips for the Methodology – Chapter 3

- Be sure to state why your method or statistical model is the correct choice and why the other choices do not fit your study.
- Describe your research question, your specific interview and survey questions, how you created the instrument, how you will test it, and how you may adapt it. If you are using an instrument from a different researcher, describe where you received it from, how it was tested before, and how it applies to your research.
- In great detail, list the population, sample and data collection method. Describe step-by-step how you will ask for permission, collect data, plan to analyze data, and how security, privacy, and confidentiality of your subjects will be protected. Describe the risks for subjects in detail and how you will mitigate them. These are points the IRB (Internal Review Board) will be looking for.

Step 11
Editing

Editing often seems the most daunting task of a dissertation. Why? Well because we always believe what we wrote is the best it can ever be!

Editing and feedback to improve writing, spelling, and sentence structure are, however, most important to improving your dissertation. Believe us, even after multiple reads, someone else will find errors and areas needing improvement!

The main areas of editing include:

1. Correct spelling
2. Correct grammar
3. Creating cohesive paragraphs (one topic per paragraph)
4. Very few instances of passive voice
5. Very few instances of direct quotes
6. Anthropomorphisms
7. And don't forget the visual editing, including page-breaks and location of tables and figures.

More Hints For Editing...

- While you are waiting for your chair and committee to review your proposal, keep working. Possible areas include adjusting the format to the requirements of the final dissertation, creating a rough outline for Chapters 4 and 5, preparing for your interviews, and more.
- There are resources online that can walk you through the set-up and adjustments to the spell-checker and grammar-checker in Word and other programs. Find a professional editor to review your proposal or prospectus, as this will help you save time in the process, because a good editor can help you avoid the known pitfalls of IRB.
- Review the IRB alignment of your study with the IRB requirements and any proposal/dissertation criteria your university has.
- Review all proposal formatting and requirements from your university and make necessary adjustments.
- Review your reference pages and the formatting your university uses. Make sure all references are complete even if it means to look for another DOI or URL!

Step 12
Overall Dissertation Content Guide

Moving on from the proposal to the dissertation stage means you received approval by your committee, your university, and the IRB board. Take time to celebrate! Perhaps go on a movie date, to dinner, or do something you have wanted to do!

Next in the dissertation process:

1. Create a copy of your proposal-file and rename it "Dissertation" Only work on the new file from now on.
2. Chapters 1 through 3 now need to be rewritten in past tense.
3. Chapters 4 and 5 have a generic structure listed in Steps 13 and 14.

Now It's On To Creating Your Dissertation...

- Whenever you are waiting for your committee or other people, keep working on your dissertation. Start changing Chapters 1-3 to past tense, re-edit your writing, and start with areas that have generic language or that you can already fill.
- Create a time-schedule for your research and put it where it's visible in your work-area. If you interview participants, establish the steps and timeframes to contact them and collect your data. If you collect data with a questionnaire, determine what your next steps are and the amount of time needed to allocate for them.
- If you are using analysis tools like NVivo or SPSS, or others, take the time (while you are waiting) to learn more about the software and how to use it. Check your university resources, the software's website, and YouTube, as well as courses offered. Knowing how to use the software may improve your studies and will definitely help you when you have to analyze the data!

Step 13
Chapter 4 - Data Analysis/Results

Chapter 4 describes your research process, including data collection and data analysis, as well as a presentation of your data collected.

In Chapter 4 you focus on your data and your findings – you present them.

Chapter 4 does not include a discussion about your findings in comparison and contrast to findings from previous research – that discussion is part of Chapter 5. The following items are listed here with numbers, but are not numbered in your dissertation.

Chapter 4: Results

1. Results
2. Demographics of Participants
3. Data Collections
4. Data Analysis
5. Theme Analysis/Statistical Analysis
6. Summary of Themes/Statistical Analysis
7. Findings
8. Summary

Tips for Data Analysis

- Describe your research process and how it took place.
- Describe how you analyzed the data.
- In great detail, list the responses to the research question or hypotheses and your findings. In qualitative research, this includes, for example, quotes from participants; in qualitative research, this includes tables of results, formulas, and other statistic representation of your data; in mixed methods studies, you will create a combination of quotes and statistic representations in support of your research question or contradictory findings.
- Discuss the reality of the qualitative, quantitative, or mixed method collection.
- Do not underestimate data analysis; as a rule of thumb, 1 minute of interview transcription takes about 10-15 minutes.
- You can find information about the processes for coding for quantitative and qualitative data analysis here: www.graduatedegreecoaches.com.

Step 14
Chapter 5 - Findings/Themes – Future Research

In Chapter 5 you summarize your study and focus on your findings, their implications, and your recommendations. Chapter 5 is often called "Findings," "Summary," or "Discussion."

This is the chapter for you to shine. Here you are finally allowed to state your own thoughts, ideas, and recommendations on your findings and their relationship to previous findings. The following items are listed here with numbers but are not numbered in your dissertation.

Chapter 5: Discussion

1. Discussion of:
    a. Limitations of the Study
    b. Implications and Findings
    c. Themes
    d. Outcome
2. Recommendations
3. Recommendation for Future Research
4. Summary

Tips for Chapter 5

- Your personal research journal you started at the onset of your dissertation process can now help you to bring ideas you had for additional research to life. Just search your notes and write comprehensive paragraphs on why and how someone should do the research in the future.
- In Chapter 5, you want to show how your research adds to existing research and the overall body of knowledge in your field.
- Be sure to include a section where you discuss research of other authors in your area and how your research agrees or disagrees with previous findings.

Step 15
Editing Again

You made it! Now the hard work begins.

1. Read your paper starting with the last paragraph and move backwards through the paper. This way your mind cannot insert what it thinks should be there!
2. Make appropriate changes.
3. Remember to update your references and appendix, as well as any tables of contents, figures, and tables.
4. Find a professional editor to also edit your paper, as they are very experienced and can provide insight you may not have considered.
5. While you are waiting for feedback from your committee, take the time to prepare your defense.
6. Take any feedback seriously! Jump over your shadow and make the requested changes!
7. Turn your document in and let us know when you are a Doctor so we can post your picture on our website!

More Editing…

- Do multiple editing rounds of your chapters; reread them in order and edit areas you changed throughout the study or that need to be explained or shortened.
- Focus on one area at a time, for example, first on sentence structure and logic, then on passive voice, then on anthropomorphisms, and so on. Focusing on too many objectives at the same time may be overwhelming!
- Reading and making annotations for 15 minutes and then applying those changes for 15 minutes will refresh your mind. Keep alternating.
- Use the search feature to find similar instances and change them throughout the document.
- Find some peers who are willing to review (parts) of your dissertation and provide you feedback – such feedback supports clear writing, as well as preparation for the oral defense.
- Take breaks; but not too long! ;)
- Be aware the dissertation is YOUR work, so make sure you put in as much effort as you can and do not rely on an editor, your committee, or your peers.

You've finished. Before you go…

Tweet/share that you finished this book.

Please star rate this book.

Reviews are solid gold to writers. Please take a few minutes to give us some itty bitty feedback on this book.

ABOUT THE AUTHORS

Friends and colleagues,

Well it is funny how in life you run into someone and you just know you will have a friend for life. On a cloudy day, one September in North Carolina, two strangers met and had one thing in common – they were both working on their doctoral degree, at the same school, in the same field of study! So one person was almost done and the other had a way to go. They agreed to work together to finish and in the process, became great friends.

Today we publish this book as a way to help others with their journey and aspire to create a worldwide community of PhD's who help others on their academic journey. You are not alone!

www.graduatedegreecoaches.com

**If You Liked This Book
You Might Also Enjoy**

- **Your Amazing Itty Bitty™ Travel Planning Book** – Rosemary Workman

- **Your Amazing Itty Bitty™ Weight Loss Book** – Suzy Prudden and Joan-Meijer-Hirschland

- **Your Amazing Itty Bitty™ Heal Your Body Book** – Patricia Garza Pinto

With many more Amazing Itty Bitty Books available in paperback and online…

www.ingramcontent.com/pod-product-compliance
Lightning Source LLC
Chambersburg PA
CBHW061304040426
42444CB00010B/2509